Paper from Wood:
Dollhouse Decisions

by Emily Sohn and Pamela Wright

Chief Content Consultant
Edward Rock
Associate Executive Director, National Science Teachers Association

NORWOOD HOUSE PRESS
Chicago, IL

Norwood House Press
PO Box 316598
Chicago, IL 60631

For information regarding Norwood House Press, please visit our website at
www.norwoodhousepress.com or call 866-565-2900.

Special thanks to: Amanda Jones, Amy Karasick, Alanna Mertens, Terrence Young, Jr.

Editors: Barbara J. Foster, Diane Hinckley
Designer: Daniel M. Greene
Production Management: Victory Productions, Inc.

Library of Congress Cataloging-in-Publication data

Sohn, Emily.

Paper from wood: dollhouse decisions / by Emily Sohn and Pam Wright.
p. cm.

Summary: "Describes how paper is made as well as the different kinds of
paper and their many different uses. Readers use scientific inquiry to learn
about when some kinds of paper are better to use than others. An activity
based on real world situations challenges them to apply what they've learned
in order to solve a puzzle"—Provided by publisher.

Includes bibliographical references and index.

ISBN-13: 978-1-59953-412-1 (library editions: alk. paper)
ISBN-10: 1-59953-412-6 (library editions: alk. paper)

1. Paper—Juvenile literature. 2. Papermaking—Juvenile literature.
I. Wright, Pamela, 1953– II. Title.

TS1105.5.S69 2011
620.1'97--dc22
2010044539

3390

Manufactured in the United States of America in North Mankato, Minnesota.

165N—012011

Contents

Note to Caregivers:

Throughout this book, many questions are posed to the reader. Some are open-ended and ask what the reader thinks. Discuss these questions with your child and guide him or her in thinking through the possible answers and outcomes. There are also questions posed which have a specific answer. Encourage your child to read through the text to determine the correct answer. Most importantly, encourage answers grounded in reality while also allowing imaginations to soar. Information to help support you as you share the book with your child is provided in the back in the **Additional Notes** section.

Words that are **bolded** are defined in the glossary in the back of the book.

What's the Best Paper Product for a Dollhouse?

Do you remember the first time you held a crayon? As soon as you could draw, you used paper. In this book, you will learn where paper comes from and how it is made. You will also enter a contest. Then you'll decide which types of paper will be the best for making a paper dollhouse.

Paper House Contest

You've been asked to enter a contest.
You will make a paper house for paper dolls.
Houses will be judged by how strong they are
and how nice they look.

Which type of paper will you use to make the
house? Here are some choices.

Choice 1: Cardboard

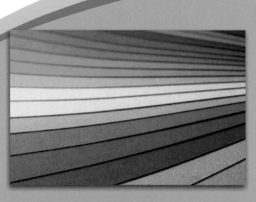

**Choice 2: Construction
Paper**

Choice 3: Paper Towel

Choice 4: Writing Paper

Before you choose,
think about these questions.

Which paper is strongest?
Which paper is easiest to shape?
Which paper is best to draw on?
Which paper is best to paint on?

Keep reading to learn more about paper. Use what you learn to make the best paper house.

Let It Rip!

Look around your home or school for paper.

See how many types you can find, besides the four dollhouse choices.

Make sure no one needs the papers anymore. Now, rip them up!

different kinds of paper

Do some papers rip more easily than others?

Put the papers that rip easily in one pile.

How else are they alike?

How are they different from the other papers?

Find a magnifying lens or a microscope.

Use it to look at the ripped edges.

What do they look like?

handmade paper as seen under a microscope

Sort the papers by color.

Now, see which have similar thickness.

Which feel alike?

How else might you put paper into groups?

How Is Paper Made?

wood chips at a papermaking plant

Before you start working on your paper house, let's learn how paper is made.

Paper doesn't grow on trees. But a lot of paper comes from trees. Trees have **fibers.** These fibers are called **cellulose.** These fibers are strong. They hold their shape well in water. Wood, which is mostly what trees are made of, has a lot of cellulose.

So, how is paper made? First, workers strip **bark** from wood.

They cut the wood into chips about the size of nickels. The wood chips are made of fibers. Next, the workers mix the chips with water. This makes soft, wet **pulp.** The pulp is sprayed onto a big screen. The water drips away and the pulp starts to dry out. The fibers start sticking together.

stripping the bark

rolls of paper

pulp

sheet of paper taken off screen

The pulp then goes through a machine that squeezes more water out. The fibers stick to each other even more. When the pulp is completely dry, paper is left.

These trees could make a lot of paper!

Did You Know?

One tree can make more than 80,000 pieces of standard 8.5-in × 11-in (21.6 cm × 28 cm) paper.

People use a lot of paper. So we need a lot of trees! Good paper companies want to make paper *and* protect trees. They plant and grow new forests to replace the trees that have been cut down to make paper and other products.

papyrus plant

papyrus paper

Connecting to History

Ancient Egyptians

Ancient people made paper, too.
These paper makers lived in Egypt.

They lived thousands of years ago. They made
paper out of tall plants. The plants are called
papyrus. These plants have long fibers.

People in Egypt cut strips from the plants.
Then, they soaked the strips in water. They put the
strips in two layers. The layers crossed each other.
They looked like a tight tic-tac-toe board.

Papyrus, left, was used to make paper scrolls like the one on the right.

The background paper is papyrus.

The people pounded the strips. This pounding pushed the strips together. When the strips dried, the people had paper.

These people did not make books the way we make books. They rolled the paper into **scrolls.** People use scrolls as decorations or as a way to communicate.

What Is Paper Like?

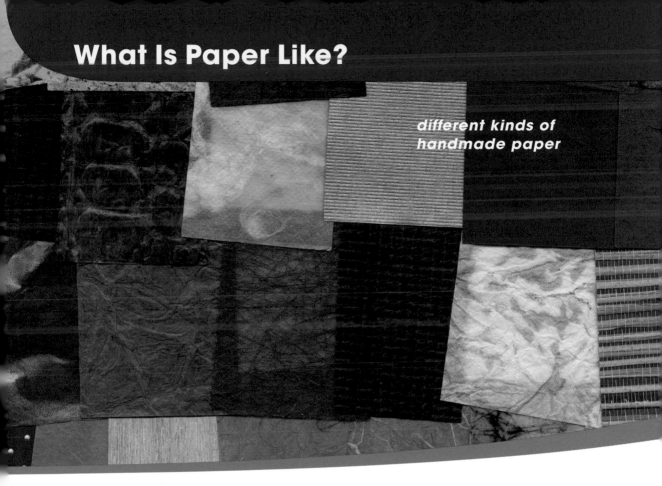

different kinds of handmade paper

Our lives are full of paper. Some paper is thick, like the side of a box. Cardboard is used a lot to make boxes. Some is thin, like a page in this book, or writing paper. Some paper is soft, like tissues. Some is rough, like paper grocery bags.

You want to make your dollhouse as strong as you can. Do you think you should use thick paper or thin paper? Which of the four papers in the contest seem strong?

Cutting paper changes its shape.

Shaping Your House

You want to win the contest. So your house needs to have a good shape. How will you form its shape? You can fold paper. You can cut it. What else can you do with paper to change its shape? How will you change your paper's shape to make your house?

Cutting Tricks

Now you know about fibers. That can help you build your house.

Here's a trick. Fold a piece of paper to make a **crease.**

Now, fold it backward. This makes the crease deeper. You might see fibers start to break apart.

The folded edge is called a crease.

Hold a ruler against the crease. Tear the paper into two pieces. The edges are nice and straight. Who needs scissors?

Fold and cut thick paper. Now, fold and cut thin paper. Which is easier?

You can cut paper or tear paper for your dollhouse. Which would you rather do?

It's time to make your house look nice. Do you want to color or paint your house? Look at your paper choices. Take a sample of each type of paper.

First, draw on each of them with a crayon. Then color on them with paint and markers. Think about the questions below.

What type of paper is best?

Which types of paper are good to write on?

Which types are good to color or paint on?

Do the paints or markers soak through some papers?

Is it easier to draw on smooth paper or rough paper?

Which kind of paper makes your art look best?

Science at Work

Papermaker

Some artists do more than paint or draw on paper—they make the paper itself. Papermakers put plant fibers in water. They stir the fibers and water into a watery mixture. The papermaker pours the mixture onto a flat mold and drains the water. What's left is a layer of fibers. The artist keeps adding layers until the sheet is the right thickness. Next, the papermaker uses a weight to press out the extra water. Finally, the sheets are hung to dry.

This woman is holding a frame for making paper.

Are you ready to make your house? Here are your paper choices again. Each has good parts, called pros. Each also has some bad parts, called cons. How do you want your house to look and how strong should it be?

Type of Paper	Pros	Cons
Cardboard	Sturdy. Easy to paint on.	Too stiff to fold. Hard to cut.
Construction Paper	Colorful.	Too dark to show some crayon or marker colors.
Paper Towel	Easy to fold and cut.	Floppy. Tears easily. Hard to paint or color on.
Writing Paper	Pretty strong. Good to draw and paint on.	May be too thin to last long.

Further Reading

Making Art with Paper, by Gillian Chapman and Pam Robson. Power Kids Press, 2007.

Trash and Recycling, by Stephanie Turnbull. Usbourne Books, 2007.

Tree, by David Burnie. DK Publishing, 2005.

Make Paper!, http://www.wipapercouncil.org/makepaper.htm

Additional Notes

The page references below provide answers to questions asked throughout the book. Questions whose answers will vary are not addressed.

Page 9: Paper can be sorted according to texture, strength, flexibility, or color.

Page 16: You can crumple it, roll it, and tear it.

Index